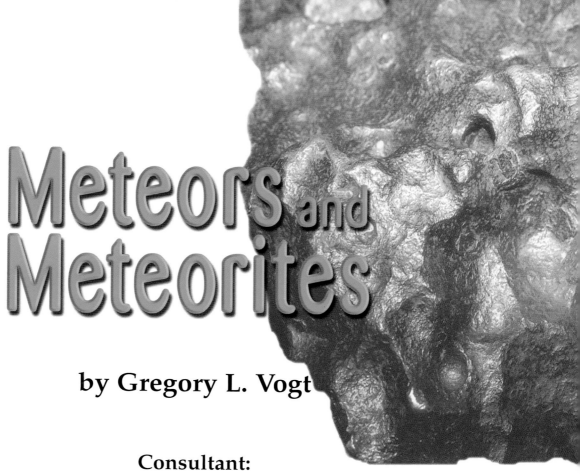

Meteors and Meteorites

by Gregory L. Vogt

Consultant:

Ralph Winrich
Former NASA Aerospace Education Specialist

Bridgestone Books
an imprint of Capstone Press
Mankato, Minnesota

Bridgestone Books are published by Capstone Press
151 Good Counsel Drive, P.O. Box 669, Mankato, Minnesota 56002
http://www.capstone-press.com

Library of Congress Cataloging-in-Publication Data
Vogt, Gregory.
    Meteors and meteorites / by Gregory L. Vogt.
    p. cm.—(The galaxy)
    Includes bibliographical references and index.
    Summary: Describes what meteors and micrometeors are, and describes the different
types of meteorites, including lunar and martian meteorites, and how meteorites form
craters.
    ISBN 0-7368-1120-6
    1. Meteors—Juvenile literature. 2. Meteorites—Juvenile literature. [1. Meteors.
2. Meteorites.] I. Title. II. Series.
QB741.5 .V64 2002
523.5'1—dc21   2001003147

Editorial Credits
Tom Adamson, editor; Karen Risch, product planning editor; Timothy Halldin,
      cover designer and interior layout designer; Jenny Schonborn, interior illustrator and
      production designer; Katy Kudela, photo researcher

Photo Credits
Anders Meibom/Antarctic Search for Meteorites Program, 12
Brian Parker/TOM STACK & ASSOCIATES, cover, 1
Digital Vision, 10
James W. Young/TMO/JPL/NASA, 4, 8
NASA, 18, 20
StockTrek/PhotoDisc/PictureQuest, 6, 16
Visuals Unlimited/Ken Lucas, 14

1 2 3 4 5 6 07 06 05 04 03 02

Table of Contents

FAST FACTS: Meteor Showers

Name	Approximate Date	Maximum Number of Meteors per Hour
Quadrantids	January 3	140
April Lyrids	April 22	10
Eta Aquarids	May 5	30
June Lyrids	June 15	10
Southern Delta Aquarids	July 29	30
Perseids	August 12	400
Aurigids	September 1	30
Orionids	October 21	30
Leonids	November 17	3,000*
Ursids	December 22	20

* The maximum number varies each year. In 1966, some people saw as many as 3,000 Leonid meteors in one hour.

Meteors and Meteorites

Meteors look like stars that are falling from the sky. They appear as a sudden bright streak in the night sky. The streak is gone in a second.

Meteors are small bits of the solar system that collide with Earth's atmosphere. The solar system is the Sun and its planets, moons, and small objects. These small objects include asteroids and comets. Meteors are made of space rock, metal, or dust.

Meteors travel quickly through space. Friction causes the meteors to heat up when they enter Earth's atmosphere. They rub against the air and get very hot. The heat causes them to burn up and give off light.

Some large meteors do not completely burn up in the atmosphere. They fall to the ground or into an ocean. A meteor that reaches Earth's surface is called a meteorite.

This meteor was from the Perseid meteor shower.

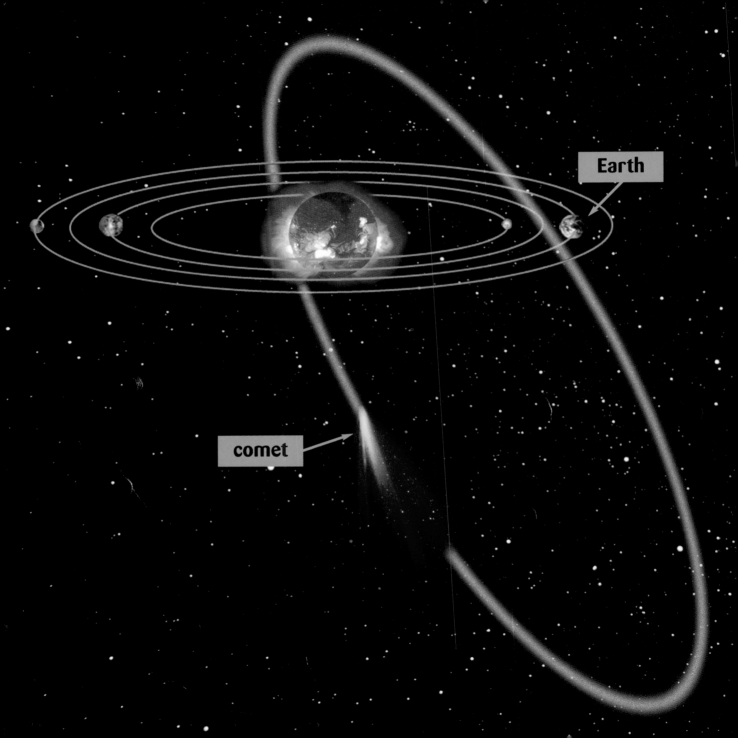

Where Do Meteors Come From?

Most meteors and meteorites are leftover matter from when the solar system formed. The Sun, planets, and moons started out as a giant cloud in space. Gravity pulled this matter together.

The Sun formed in the middle of this cloud. Lumps of matter formed the planets and moons. Leftover matter became smaller pieces called asteroids and comets. Asteroids are like small planets made of rock. Comets are chunks of ice mixed with sand and dust.

Meteors come from pieces of asteroids and comets. Asteroids sometimes bump into each other. Small pieces break off and can become meteors. When comets come close to the Sun, some of the ice melts. The melting ice releases dust and sand. These pieces become micrometeors. Micrometeors are very small meteors.

Some meteors come from the dust of a comet's orbit. The dust enters Earth's atmosphere when Earth crosses the comet's orbit.

Micrometeors

Micrometeors come from the dust and sand mixed in comet ice. Some of the ice melts as comets approach the Sun. Dust and sand are released in space. The dust particles enter the atmosphere as Earth passes through the dust trail.

Micrometeors travel through space at very high speeds. A micrometeor traveling 40 to 50 miles (64 to 80 kilometers) per second is dangerous. If it strikes a spacecraft, it can blast a hole. The spacecraft can be damaged or destroyed if hit by enough micrometeors.

Spacecraft designers put shields on the outside of spacecraft. The shields are built in layers. A micrometeor may get through the first shield. But it will not get through the layers underneath.

These meteors were caused by the dust trail of comet Tempel-Tuttle.

Space Walking

Astronauts go on space walks to repair spacecraft. They wear bulky space suits when they step outside the spacecraft. A space suit is like a suit of armor. Space suits protect astronauts from being hit by micrometeors. The inside of the space suit has air for the astronaut to breathe.

The space suit is made of the same material as bulletproof vests. It has many layers of tough white nylon fabric. Micrometeors cannot get through the tough fabric.

Astronauts also wear a hard helmet. The helmet has a clear plastic window in front to look through. Micrometeors travel very fast. But they cannot punch through the helmet. They may make a bang and a small pit in the helmet's surface.

Space suits protect astronauts when they go on space walks.

Searching for Meteorites

Two boys found a meteorite one summer evening in Noblesville, Indiana. They were standing in a yard. The boys heard a whistling sound and then a thud. The small meteorite landed a few feet away from them. It made a shallow hole in the ground.

The two boys were very lucky. Few people get to see a meteorite when it falls. Earth's surface is 71 percent water. Most meteorites sink in the oceans.

Meteorites that hit land can look like regular rocks. Many meteorites are never found unless someone sees them fall.

Antarctica is one place where it is easy to find meteorites. This continent is mostly covered with ice and snow. Meteorites are dark. They are easy to spot lying on top of white snow and ice. Every summer, scientists go to Antarctica to search for meteorites.

Scientists search for meteorites in Antarctica. The dark meteorites are easy to find on the white snow.

Types of Meteorites

About 30,000 meteorites that weigh 4 ounces (100 grams) or more fall to the ground every year. People find only a few of these meteorites.

Meteorites can be divided into three main types. Stony meteorites are made of rock. They may have some metal such as iron mixed in with the rock. Most meteorites are stony meteorites. Iron meteorites are mostly iron metal mixed with nickel metal. Only about one in 20 meteorites is an iron meteorite. The third type of meteorite is a stony-iron meteorite. It is half rock and half metal. This type of meteorite is rare.

Meteorites can be difficult to recognize. They look similar to Earth rocks. Iron meteorites are heavier than Earth rocks. Stony meteorites have a glassy crust. This crust forms from the heat created when a meteorite falls through Earth's atmosphere.

This stony-iron meteorite was found in Wyoming.

About 50,000 years ago, a large meteorite struck the Arizona desert. The meteorite was 100 feet (30 meters) across. It weighed about 1 million tons (900,000 metric tons).

The meteorite caused a huge explosion. After the dust settled, there was a bowl-shaped hole called a crater. The crater is three-fourths of a mile (1.2 kilometers) wide and 570 feet (174 meters) deep. The rock around the crater rim was bent upward by the blast.

The explosion scattered small pieces of the meteorite in and around the crater. The pieces were made mostly of iron mixed with some nickel.

Large meteorites have struck Earth many times. Most strikes happened millions of years ago. Wind and water have erased the craters. Only a few hundred craters can be found on Earth. Most craters are barely visible. Some craters are filled with water.

A meteorite struck the Arizona desert about 50,000 years ago to form this crater.

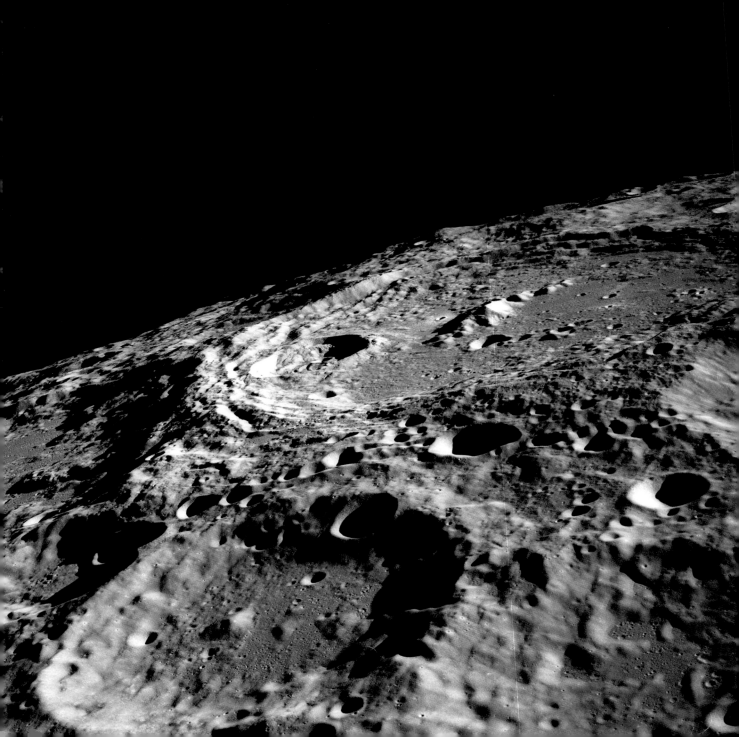

Craters on the Moon

The Moon's surface is covered with millions of craters. They last millions of years because there is no wind or water to wear them away.

Craters on the Moon are many sizes. Some craters are small like the pits made in dirt when raindrops fall. Other craters are many miles or kilometers across. Meteorites have hit the Moon many times. Some craters cover other craters.

Large meteorites create the largest craters on the Moon. The impact is like throwing a pebble into a pond. The pebble makes a dent in the water's surface. But the water fills back in right away. When a large meteorite hits the Moon, the impact creates very high temperatures. Some of the Moon rock and parts of the meteorite melt. The rock acts like the water in a pond. Some of the melted rock fills in and makes a mound in the middle of the crater. The rock then hardens. Large craters often have mountains in the middle.

These large craters on the Moon have mountains in the middle.

Lunar and Martian Meteorites

Scientists have found some meteorites that did not come from deep space. Some meteorites came from the Moon and Mars.

Scientists recognize lunar meteorites because they compare them to Moon rocks. Between 1969 and 1972, 12 astronauts walked on the Moon. They brought many Moon rocks back to Earth. The lunar meteorites look like these Moon rocks.

Robot spacecraft have studied rocks on Mars. Martian meteorites look like the rocks on Mars.

Scientists think asteroids or comets struck Mars and the Moon. They blasted out big craters. Some of the rocks from their surfaces were thrown out into space. They eventually fell to Earth.

Scientists find the martian meteorites especially interesting. Some of the meteorites may show evidence of life. The rocks may have fossils. If the scientists are right, there may have been life on Mars.

This martian meteorite was found in Antarctica. Scientists think it may show signs of past life.

Hands On: Mapping Meteors

Meteor showers occur several times each year. You can draw a map of the meteors' paths to find out which direction they are coming from.

What You Need

Red cellophane
Flashlight
Rubber band
Blanket

Clipboard
Paper
Pencil
An adult to go with you

What You Do

1. Find the date of the next meteor shower by looking at the Fast Facts on page 4.
2. Wrap red cellophane around the lens of the flashlight. Hold it there with a rubber band. The red light will help your eyes stay adjusted to the dark.
3. Choose an area where the sky is dark at night and find a comfortable spot to lay out your blanket.
4. Watch the sky for meteors. Draw a map of the stars in the area where you see meteors. Draw a line for the path of the meteor and put an arrow on it to show which direction it went.
5. Each time you see a meteor, draw another line on your map.

When you have several meteor streaks on your map, try to determine where they came from. Compare your map to a map of the star constellations in the same area of the sky. From what constellation did your meteors appear to fall?

Words to Know

asteroid (ASS-tuh-roid)—a large space rock that orbits the Sun
atmosphere (AT-muhss-feehr)—the mixture of gases that surrounds some planets
comet (KOM-it)—a chunk of ice and rock that orbits the Sun
crater (KRAY-tur)—a hole in the ground made by a meteorite
fossil (FOSS-uhl)—the remains of an animal or plant preserved as rock
friction (FRIK-shuhn)—the force created by a moving object as it rubs against something else
gravity (GRAV-uh-tee)—a force that pulls objects together
impact (IM-pakt)—the striking of one object against another
meteor (MEE-tee-ur)—a streak of light in the sky caused by a piece of rock or dust that enters Earth's atmosphere
meteorite (MEE-tee-ur-rite)—a piece of space rock that strikes a planet or a moon
meteor shower (MEE-tee-ur SHOU-er)—an event when many meteors can be seen in a short time period

Read More

Gallant, Roy A. *Comets, Asteroids, and Meteorites.* Kaleidoscope. Tarrytown, N.Y.: Benchmark Books, 2001.

Kerrod, Robin. *Asteroids, Comets, and Meteors.* Planet Library. Minneapolis: Lerner, 2000.

Vogt, Gregory. *Asteroids, Comets, and Meteors.* Our Universe. Austin, Texas: Steadwell Books, 2001.

Useful Addresses

Canadian Space Agency
6767 Route de l'Aéroport
Saint-Hubert, QC J3Y 8Y9
Canada

NASA Headquarters
Washington, DC 20546-0001

Internet Sites

ANSMET—The Antarctic Search for Meteorites
http://www.cwru.edu/affil/ansmet
Comets and Meteor Showers
http://comets.amsmeteors.org
Terrestrial Impact Craters
http://www.solarviews.com/eng/tercrate.htm

Index